JEFF BECK
Super Rock Guitarist

This Folio ©1991 International Music Publications/Rittor Music Europe Ltd.
Published by International Music Publications/Rittor Music Europe Ltd.
Southend Road, Woodford Green, Essex IG8 8HN/24 Broomgrove Gardens, Edgware, Middx. HA8 5SJ
Text and Transcription copyright: Rittor Music Inc. Tokyo Japan.
Translation by: Takako Imai and Alan Hobbs
Printed by: Panda Press · Haverhill · Suffolk CB9 8PR

CONTENTS

JEFF BECK'S GUITAR SOUND

I think it is impossible to associate any one fixed sound with Jeff Beck. It seems to be a case of what ever suits the moment best and this capacity for variation is one of the traits makes his electric guitar playing so striking. Guitarists like Ritchie Blackmore, Carlos Santana, Eric Clapton, Larry Carlton, Eddie Van Halen, Mark Knopfler and Tom Scholz are all fine, inventive electric players but all of them go for a particular guitar sound from a certain guitar /amp set-up, a sound that is inevitably associated with them as individuals.

However it must be said that Beck shares more than a casual affinity with the Fender Stratocaster, especially when he's on stage. When I saw him in Japan in the late '70s he was using a '54 sunburst Strat with unmodified electrics plugged into a customised Marshall stack. He also possesses two white Strats from the 60s, one of which is mounted with either a Schecter or Seymour Duncan assembly.

The albums "Blow by Blow" and "Wired" feature a range of effects that at that time were relatively new, such as the 'talking modulator', 'octave divider' and 'ring modulator' (or 'frequency analyser') as well as his customised fuzz box. The resulting guitar sounds from these two albums were nevertheless distinctive and crafted, never really veering off into pure experimentation for it's own sake. The feeling is that Beck is deliberately looking for a combination of sounds that are both striking in themselves and together provide a contrast that always adds a quality of freshness to his guitar sound. Specific sounds, especially on "Wired", tend to mark out each piece just as they make passages within the pieces stand out from one another. Even within any one guitar sound Beck always seems to be searching for variations on that sound, changing pickups over, sometimes from one chord to another, resetting tone controls, bringing in bottleneck and tremolo arm or changing pickups over in mid-song to another guitar; the impression is that guitar sound for him is a fluid thing, never fixed, and needs a kind of ceaseless coaxing to keep it's impact alive. It also shows that Beck constantly listens to what he plays, that he plays by ear and not by contrived formulas. Tracks like 'She's A Woman', 'Diamond Dust', 'Goodbye Pork Pie Hat' and 'Come Dancing' give a good illustration of this point.

The sound expresses the emotion in the playing as much as, if not more than, the phrases themselves and this seems to be equally true for Carlos Santana's playing as for Beck's. However, unlike Santana with his polished and sensitive, warm sounding Les Paul, Beck doesn't appear to turn his nose up at any particular sound. He does not strive after a consciously 'beautiful' guitar sound like Santana and he is never precious about his sound. Even the poignancy of the lilting guitar on 'Definitely Maybe' is undermined just a touch by smile raising, if subtle inflections on the wah-wah pedal. And the playing still loses none of it's impact. That Jeff Beck kept his liking for gritty, dirty R&B sounds right through to the jazzier times is clear on numbers like 'Scatterbrain' and 'Air Blower' or the tremolo vandalism on the solo in 'Freeway Jam'.

Perhaps here is a clue to the endless personnel changes in a string of bands. His approach, unlike Jimmy Page or Brian May, is too individual to seriously set about the job of moulding his sound to fit in with an ensemble sound. Fickle and reckless in his playing, Beck somehow always sounds best soaring above the backdrop of the band, creating his own moods and atmospheres with the kind of spontaneity that demands a lot of space.

To copy such a sound is not so simple, and to try and recreate every single nuance might make for an instructive exercise but would prove pretty pointless as a vehicle to express his playing. It goes, I think, against the spirit in which he himself has made those sounds. A far better means of bringing these examples of his playing to life is to grasp Beck's principle behind his endeavours and follow his example in your own approach.

CHRONICLE OF EQUIPMENT

YARDBIRDS:

1960 white Fender Telecaster, rosewood neck, given by Page as a present; 1952 white Fender Esquire, maple neck, bought from John Walker of The Walker Brothers; 1958 sunburst Gibson Les Paul standard (rarely used).

JEFF BECK GROUP FIRST PERIOD:

1958 Gibson Les Paul, bought from Rick Nielsen of Cheap Trick but later stolen; 1966 white Fender Stratocaster, rosewood neck, used in Beck, Bogart, Appice; 1950 white Fender Telecaster, maple neck.

SECOND PERIOD:

1954 model natural finish Fender Stratocaster, maple neck changed later to rosewood neck.

BECK, BOGART, APPICE:

1955 black Gibson Les Paul, single coil pickup, gold top model (rumoured to be one of the first Les Paul Deluxes released).

SOLO CAREER:

1960 white Fender Stratocaster, rosewood neck, gift from John McLaughlin, changed assembly from Seymour Duncan to Schecter; 1954 white Fender Stratocaster, maple neck; 1950 white Fender Telecaster, maple neck, pickups changed to Gibson PAF humbuckers; 1952 model white Fender Esquire, (manufactured 1955) maple neck, Roland GR guitar synth.

AMPS:

Vox AC30; Vox Super Beatle top, Marshall 50w, 100w and 200w, all old models from 1960s and customised to increase volume, still uses 100w and 200w amps; Sunn Colloseum top (2nd period of J.B. Group) with Univox speaker cabinet, used from Beck, Bogart, Appice until Jan Hammer Group. Other amps include Fender and Ampeg plus several small combos.

EFFECTS:

Vox Tone Bender (custom made); Coloursound Overdrive (customised); Boss OD-1 overdrive; Vox Cry Baby wah-wah; De Armand volume pedal; MXR Phase 100 phaser; MXR flanger; Ticobrahe pedal flanger; Maestro Echoplex echo unit; Roland Space Echo RE 201; MXR 10 band equaliser; Boss Chorus Ensemble; Boss Stereovox Talking Modulator (probably custom made); Coloursound Ring Modulator; Coloursound Octivider or Octavair ; Leslie Cabinet (for studio use only).

A FEW FOOTNOTES

Beck's phrasing and choice of notes is based, even throughout the period that saw him embracing the jazz tradition, on the form and harmony of his first big musical influence, the American blues players, whose music began to filter through to England in the '50s and '60s. This was the first musical vocabulary for most of the emerging rock players of his generation. Although I think everyone will be familiar with the very basic nuts and bolts of rock guitar, I have written out a few examples that briefly illustrate these points.

If you glance at Score Sample 1, I've sketched out the opening bars of 'Highways' to show how this and countless other licks and phrases are based upon a five note or 'pentatonic' scale. If you find you are not well acquainted with this, I would suggest running through this passage and trying to make other riffs and tunes out of it. Beck is also fond of inserting just about any notes he can get away with, an affection shared by most jazz players. Sometimes these are traditional blues 'blue' notes, at other times they are simply unrelated to the key and work because of the way they are phrased and because their delivery is confident. In Score Sample 2 I've included an example of this taken from the Beck, Bogart, Appice number 'Lady'. In fact the examples are numerous.

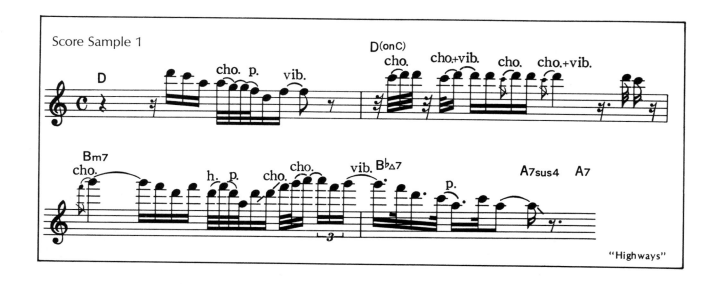

"Highways"

"Lady"

These kind of phrases are very simple but, like any 'simple' music, delivering it with some passion and conviction as Beck himself does is not such a pushover. It is also easy to get rather too 'position-bound' when playing pentatonic scales as they make such a neat pattern on the fretboard. This will ruin and stiffen all attempts to create good phrases as well as preventing the player from developing perhaps the most important ability: being able to play by ear. Score Sample 3 from 'Come Dancing' and 'Sophie' reflects how you can break up fixed patterns with wide intervals and sequences. Beck likes to use all of the fretboard and never lets himself get polarised into any one area.

Rhythm is another vital element in Beck's phrasing and

I've taken three examples, from 'Come Dancing', 'Blue Wind' and 'Lady' for Score Sample 4 as being strong in this area. You will naturally need to hear these examples and to try them out for yourself on the guitar. These are not the best examples, there are too many good ones, but they are direct and uncomplicated illustrations of these basic key points.

It is also important for a sound appreciation of Beck's style, to listen to *how* his playing has developed over the years. In many ways his playing has become simpler and more focused, happily abandoning the tricky sounding show off lines of the classic 'Jeff's Boogie' for a more melodic and memorable approach to his craft.

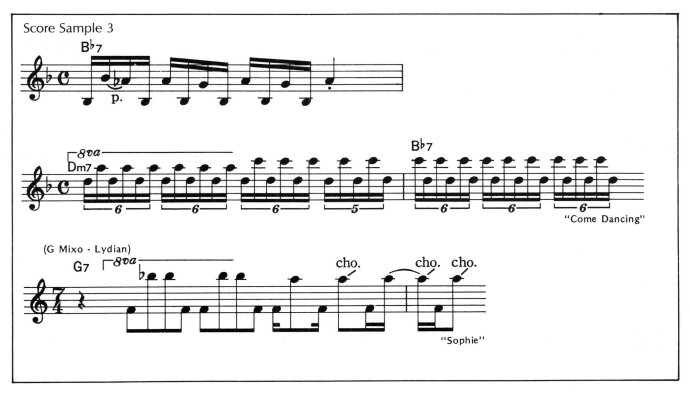

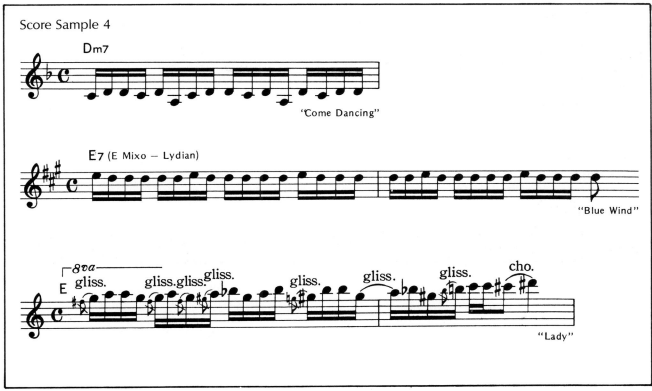

BLUE WIND

STRUCTURE

[A]: intro section featuring 4 bar theme transcribed onto Guitar II part.

[B]: second distinctive theme of piece played in Guitar I part, punctuated by 2 bar riff from Guitar II.

[C]: guitar solo over same E7→A7→E7 harmony as [B] section.

[D]: synth solo.

[E]: guitar solo, still over E7 and A7.

[F]: synth solo.

[G]: guitar solo.

[H]: synth solo.

⊕ Coda: Back to intro theme with guitar and synth ad-libbing over the top.

GENERAL ASPECTS

The guitar lines don't really employ any outstanding or unusual approaches from a technical point of view. Worth noting are the low bends on the bottom three strings on the two riffs played by Guitar II in sections [A] and [B], and the seven consecutive bars from [E] which contain a passage made up entirely of harmonics. As always, Beck favours plenty of bent notes in his phrasing but most are within a single tone and high up on the fretboard. The most important point is probably to keep a strong, rolling rhythm going to the repeated riffs in the second guitar part.

GUITAR SOUND

At times, if you listen hard, occasional shifts to a richer guitar tone seem to suggest a Les Paul in there somewhere but overall a Stratocaster is the ideal instrument for the job. To basically recreate Beck's own spectrum of guitar sounds it's important to go for a variety of tones which is best achieved with some imaginative use of effect pedals. However, he does appear to be switching back and forth to other guitars on the album so, a more practical guideline would be to take Beck's lead on the live performances of 'Blue Wind' and use different effects on alternate phrases. This gives a kind of unique flavour to the the various lines, lending a more imposing impact to the phrasing, as well as livening up the band sound.

PLAYING TIPS

①: On these semitone bends (or 'chokes') low down on the 5th and 6th strings don't forget to bend the string up across the fretboard, towards the top E string, allowing plenty of space on the fretboard. Finger the C# at the 4th fret/5th string with the ring finger.

[C]: On the album there are three different guitar tones used in the first 16 bars and the last 3 bars.

[E]: The harmonics occurring across the 1st and 2nd bars marked ② are all 'natural' harmonics and can be easily played over the fret wires of the 12th, 7th and 5th frets on the bottom E string. From ③: the D note on the score is also a natural harmonic and can found just below the 3rd fret wire from the nut end of the neck. There are 2 harmonics here between these two fret wires. If you go too near the 2nd fret you will produce an E note, too far in the opposite direction and it will be a B. In any event, a light touch with the left hand and a sharp pluck with the pick is needed to get it ringing clearly, like all overtones not found on the 5th, 7th and 12th frets.

④: The E and B harmonics in this bar and the following bar lie on either side of the D over the 3rd fret/6th string as detailed in ③: above.

⑤: The phrase beginning on the B→D bend over one and a half tone bend after the furious tremolo'd harmonics is somewhat tricky and might benefit from being practised separately. The rapid change over is difficult to hit timingwise. This bluesy phrase needs to be emphatic and drag slightly on the beat with heavy down strokes on the plectrum. It's often a basic mistake to rush lines and phrases as this usually ends up sounding just hectic instead of exciting. A good deal more confidence is needed to really squeeze out the beat and linger over the notes in a phrase than to simply thrash things out in a flurry of notes that have neither expression nor rhythm.

N.B.: Section [B] Guitar II part, bars 1, 2, 5, 6, 9, 10, 13, 14, when playing the muted bottom E string on the second time repeat, do this only on the 1st beat if you wish to stick exactly to the record.

BLUE WIND

Music by JAN HAMMER

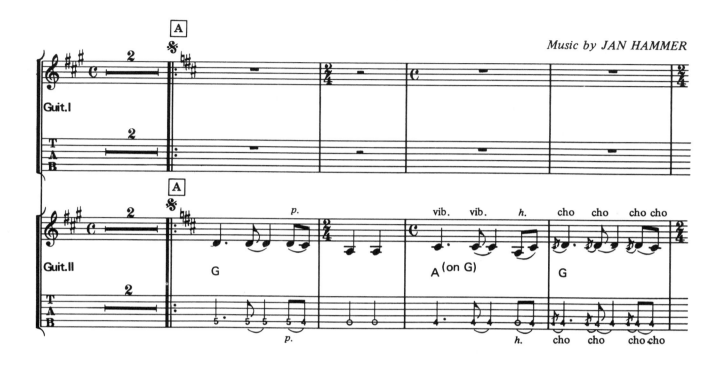

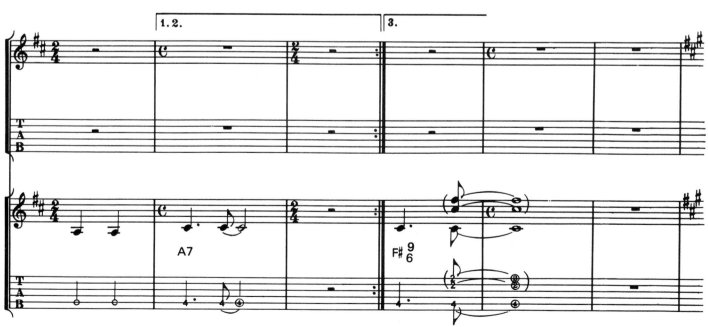

COME DANCING

STRUCTURE

[A]: 3 bar drum intro.
[B]: Guitar entry on jerky, off beat rhythm.
[C]: Entry of electric piano and horn section.
[D]: 8 bar chorus type theme featuring brass strongly.
[E]: Guitar solo.
[F]: Repeat of chorus theme with synth solo over the top.
[G]: 12 bar passage introduces new theme.
[H]: Electric piano solo.
[I]: Guitar solo.
[J]: Synth solo for 16 bars on chorus theme.
[K]: Closing bars on main Dm7→B♭7 funk beat to fade out.

GENERAL ASPECTS

GENERAL ASPECTS In sections [B] and [C] the guitar concentrates on back up work with scratchy punctuation on fragmented chords and muted licks that infuse the funk rhythm into a spiky, clownish beat. You should hold the pick lightly in the fingers to give a flexible and delicate attack to the picking strokes. This should help to get the eccentric rhythm nicely. In contrast the two guitar solos in [E] and [I], although keeping the sharp edge on the beat, have a strong decisive kind of attack in the right hand.

GUITAR SOUND

GUITAR SOUND The guitar on this track is either a Strat or a Telecaster throughout. In section [E], the first of the two guitar solos, Beck uses an octave-divider to give the impression of doubling-up on the phrases. From the two heavily stated C→D chokes on the 5th string, six bars before the synth takes over, he piles on the already present distortion to lead the solo out with a toppy fuzz tone.

PLAYING TIPS

The scratchy pick work in the back-up lines that signal the guitar entry in and throughout section [B] needs to create a jagged kind of bounce on the sixteen beat funk back-beat. Into the following section, [C], as the electric piano and horns start playing the main riff, the brush strokes on the guitar start to include muted strings as single notes or half-dampened chords. Keep the attack light and delicate with your the right hand when playing this, strumming from the wrist only rather than sweeping movements of the forearm, so that guitar really dances on the rhythm.

[B]: One more small word of advice for approaching the guitar part here: I think it's best to avoid labouring too much over the score note for note when trying to recreate Beck's side work. It might be more effective, as well as more enjoyable, to take out the individual phrases and work them up until you get the feel for them. You can then stick them back in the order that appears on the transcription or juggle them around a little as Beck himself, always a very spontaneous player, would doubtless do.

[B]: The fragmented chordwork is worth giving a little thought too if you want to understand how it functions harmonically. As you can hear, it tends to imply the chord progression rather than explicitly spell it out with full chords. Take a look at the first 2 bars: the two note chord consisting of F and C is put into a D minor context with help naturally from the bass line thumping out the D root. Beck just needs to put together the 3rd and 7th intervals of the chord to produce a Dm7 harmony. Similarly the two notes A♭ and D in the next bar produce, in conjunction with the bass, a B♭7 chord which again is built on the 3rd and 7th intervals. The little E♭→D figure that follows just extends the B♭7 chord with a suspended 4th note resolving down onto the major 3rd interval. In other words the chord could be described as B♭7sus4→B♭7, a very common progression appearing in all fields of music.

①: For these harmonised bends finger the A♭ at the 6th fret/4th string with the index finger and the E♭ at the 8th fret/3rd string with the ring finger, bending the two strings together.

[C]: The small 'x' at the top of the stems on the score and guitar tab indicate what the Japanese call 'air-picking' or muting the string and picking it. Just hold the previous note played and dampen the string with the right hand.

②: This two note slide or glissando down a semitone and back on A♭ and D should be fingered with the index and ring fingers respectively. Be sure to return squarely on the beat.

[E]: There's nothing particularly difficult as far as technique goes about this solo but without a good feel for the spiky funk rhythm that underlines every phrase, it will fall a bit . It is also important to highlight and put across the rhythmic variations that occur from one phrase to another which add some nice little touches to this solo.

③: A neat example of how to make a phrase out of a simple arpeggio: the broken two note chords that form the guitar back up have been shaped into this lick with the addition of a few blue passing notes. As you can see the first bar traces out the same root, 3rd and 7th intervals of a Dm7 harmony, starting on the choked 7th note C through D to F, while in the following bar, a figure centred around A♭, B♭ and D sketches out a B♭7 chord (see notes above). Be sure to mute the open D string with the right hand at the beginning of this part.

④: These rows of 16th beat sextuplets look more formidable than they are. As you can hear on the album they are not too speedy but they provide an effective contrast in terms of rhythm.

⑤: Another example of a one and a half tone bend, going from D→F high up on the 2nd string. It also works nicely as the second of three accentuated bends that each trail off into a kind of 'answering' phrase while moving in an ascending sequence. Listen to it on the album. It begins with the C→D bend at the start of the previous bar and runs through this and the following couple of bars. Although Beck muffs it a little, it forms a nice example of solid blues type phrasing.

⑥: There are two continuous trills in this bar on C & D and B♭ & C. Use the index and ring fingers to play them, moving down two frets from 8/10 to 6/8 for the second trill. Naturally if you have a tremolo arm then you can depress the arm while holding a continuous hammer-on/pull-off. It doesn't really sound that way though on the record.

COME DANCING

Music by NARADA MICHAEL WALDEN

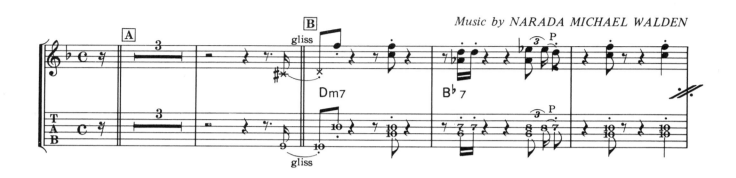

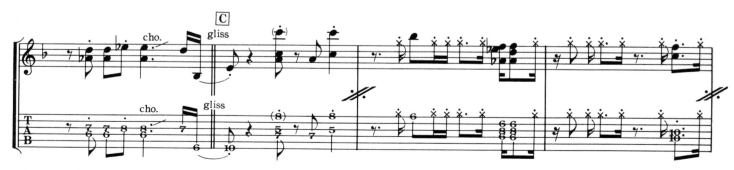

Synth Solo
8 bars

— 29 —

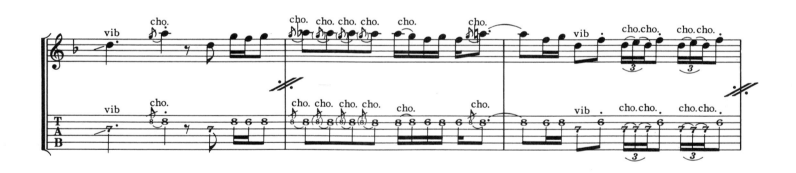

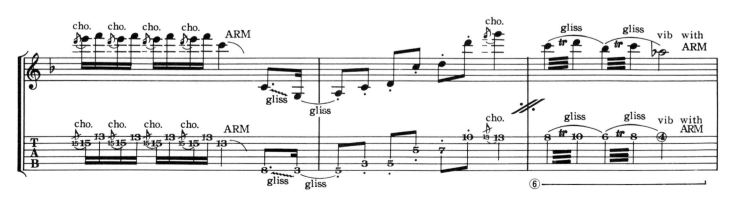

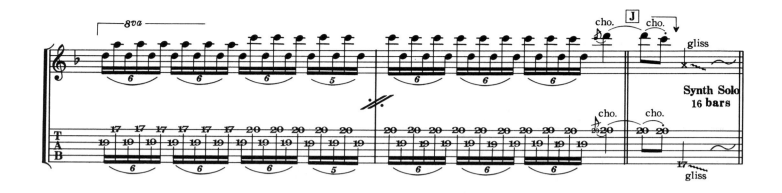

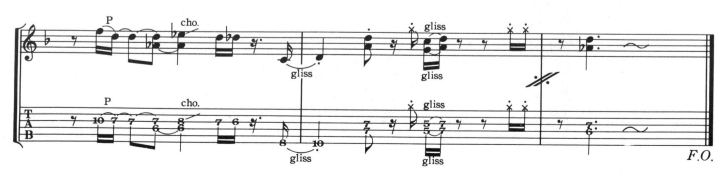

SOPHIE

STRUCTURE

Intro: Piano introduces 7/8 time signature and basic chord sequence for 6 bars.

[A]: Guitar enters with first theme.

[B] & [C]: Time signature changes to 4/4 but keeps irregular rhythm with loose variation on first theme.

[D]: Time signature to 7/4 with new riff.

[E]: Synth solo.

[F]: Same riff and pattern as [D].

[G]: Same as intro.

[H]: Same as [A].

[I]: Same as [B].

[J]: Same as [C].

[K]: Same as [D].

[L]: Same as [E] but switching over to guitar solo and then developing into guitar/synth exchange of phrases.

[M]: Ending.

GENERAL ASPECTS

This number is rather complicated as a series of interesting but dubiously related passages are welded together, building block fashion, giving the music a stop/start feel. Owing to this distinctly unhomogenous approach, the form of the piece also seems confused. However as you can see from the summary above, it does have a set pattern which consists essentially of three main ideas, each one based upon the three different time signatures that occur in the number: 7/8, 4/4 and 7/4. This sequence is then repeated a second time. Odd beat time signatures like 7/8 are awkward to play in at first and the beats have to be counted out until you get the feel of the particular rhythm you are using and can place the off beats and accents without making it sound forced. In fact in this piece the rhythm of the 4/4 section is actually far more irregular than either of the two quite straightforward rhythms in the 7/8 and 7/4 sections. As anyone reading this book probably has the main riffs and melodies of this number firmly in their head, they will in any case tend to tackle these irregular beat patterns in an instinctive way, and this is the best approach. If you don't know this track then I think you should listen to it a few times before trying to glean the phrases from the score.

The harmony is also complex, too complex for a serious analysis here, as it is built around the chromatic shifts in the main themes but mostly it involves either pairs of IVm7→Im7 chords or an unharmonised passage based on a riff: in the opening [A] section this IVm7→Im7 pattern shifts up via a semitone step to 'brighten' on a major and then fall back down; section [B] makes a kind of loose variation on [A] both in terms of harmony and melody: the melody shape remains similar and falls onto a 3 note

pause while the harmony retains its IVm7-Im7 pairings with some semitone shifts. The sections built around a riff are harmonised by a single chord as in the 7/4 part.

The guitar work itself here is not too difficult. A tremolo arm is really required to do justice to the opening [A] section and some strong wailing bends are needed to get the striking guitar theme in [D] and [F] to come across.

GUITAR SOUND

There are at least three basic kinds of sound used: a very soft edged distortion, a shrill treble (bridge pickup) and a ring modulator. It is as always impossible to say for certain whether a Les Paul has been used for some passages as well as a Strat. Sections [A] and [B] feature a Strat switched over to the first pickup or neck pickup with a parallel stereo lead, one jack connected straight to the amp for a clean sound and the other to various effects. It is then possible to mix these sounds together. Don't forget to switch over to the middle pick up for a grittier tone on the third and last repeat of the theme. [C], [D] and [F] are basically Strat sounds with distortion, with the bridge pick up on for the the main theme in [D] and [L] features the ring modulator.

PLAYING TIPS

[A]: One way of handling the 7/8 time signature if it's causing any problems is to divide it into one group of regular beats and one group of irregular beats. In all there are 6 bars to the theme. So as the chord changes fall always on the 4th beat, you could count out one bar of 3/8 and one of 4/8, (although 4/8 and 3/8 might fit the melody better on the first bar). The thing that needs to be grasped is simply the accented 4th beat. Far easier is simply to know how the theme goes in your head and let your intuition guide you.

①: The bent notes here are just textural devices to make the notes howl a little in contrast to the previous bar. So, they should not be overdone. The E♭ on the 8th fret/3rd string can be fingered with the middle finger for the semitone bend to E♮ , the B after with the ring finger and the D♭ on the 6th fret/3rd string with the index finger. The following bar then requires the tremolo arm to alter the notation.

②: From here on the tremolo arm is used throughout the phrase to add tension to the melody, especially as it comes to rest on the three note descending lick. Depress the tremolo arm after sounding the second note, D, and pick the following B before allowing the arm to return to position. This kind of method will create a nice sigh on the note.

③: The opening two bars at [D] employ natural harmonics running down the 3rd string at the 12th, 7th, 5th and 3rd frets with some tremolo arm on the last one. These harmonics want to ring out clearly above the ascending riff underneath. Give the string a sharp twang and don't release your left hand finger too soon; correctly timing the split second release of the left hand after the note has been sounded makes for strong ringing harmonics over any fret of the instrument.

④ : Strong, well judged bends and good timing to land the notes on the beat will make this riff sing out as it does when Beck play it. When practising this line (or any rhythmic passage) keep a tempo going no matter how slow.

⑤: See point ②:. As the E at the beginning of the bar does not involve depressing the tremolo arm, take care that the tremolo arm on the following E♭ is on target.

⑥: This passage of repeated sextuplet figures should not present too many problems as the low action of most electric guitars facilitates this kind of lick built around continuous pull-offs. The timing though does need to be bang on and the pull-offs cleanly delivered, with each note standing out clearly if a mess of blurred and sloppy phrasing is to be avoided. Isolating one of these sextuplets and running through it could be a good way of tightening it up should it prove troublesome.

SOPHIE

Music by NARADA MICHAEL WALDEN

G7 (G Mixo-Lydian)

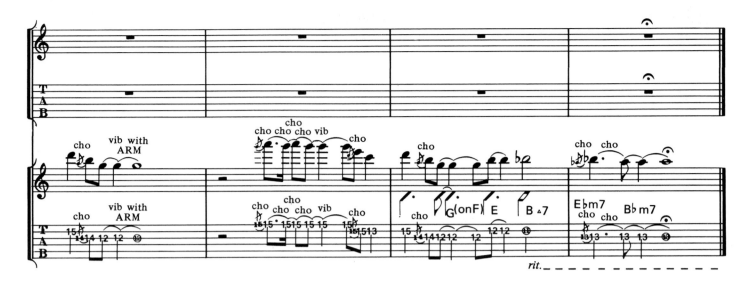

PLAY WITH ME

STRUCTURE

Intro: First 4 bars clavinet introduces riff then joined by back-up guitar.

[A]: Guitar II enters with verse type theme.

[B]: Bridge type passage over single Dm7 harmony with synth solo.

[C]: Second guitar theme forming highlight of piece.

[D]: Same as intro.

[A]→ coda: Features long synth solo, then through to the Dm7 passage and coda, a repetition of [C], and fade out.

GUITAR SOUND

Again Beck opts for a very toppy, wailing tone similar to the guitar that plays the high unison riff in section [D] of 'Sophie'. Possibly he uses a Les Paul for the bright phrases over the clavinet riff. For amplification, Beck was tending to leave his favoured combination of a Marshall top with Fender Dual Showman speakers for Sunn equipment at around the time "Wired" was recorded. So, Sunn amps are probably the sound source for this and other numbers from that album.

GENERAL ASPECTS

For the most part a very straightforward piece of jazz-funk in the mould of tunes like 'Come Dancing'. Needless to say, injecting some strident funk into the short and vocal guitar riffs that highlight the music is the most important thing to go for.

PLAYING TIPS

The main theme of sections [A] and [B] is played in unison with the synth. Therefore clean and accurate notation is called for, otherwise any fluffed notes will clang against the parallel synth lines. This is a little easier said than done as the simple blues riff of a melody contains a lot of high bends.

①: The fingering here can be a bit awkward. To play this smoothly I found that the most practical fingering is as follows: the D at the 7th fret/3rd string play with the index finger and bend up to E♭, the B♭ on the 4th string with the middle finger and the D→E♭ bend at the 10th fret/1st string with the little finger. If bending on the first string with the little finger doesn't sound very appealing, the only other way I can think of is to play the lower D→E♭ bend at the 12th fret/4th string with the ring finger, move down to the 8th fret with the index finger and play the high D→E♭

bend on the 1st string with the ring finger. If you can find a more comfortable way then good luck. In any case don't forget to stop the D note (before the B♭) sharply as it is 'staccato'.

②: This backing riff which echoes the clavinet can be played in the first position, i.e. with the index, middle, ring and little fingers corresponding to all notes occurring respectively on the 1st, 2nd, 3rd, and 4th frets. If the little two note chord of E♭ and B♭ on the second beat seems uncomfortable fingered with the little finger on the E♭ and the ring on the B♭ then try substituting the middle and index fingers. The index that barred the first three strings at the first fret for the chord on A, C, and F will slide up up to the 3rd fret/3rd string easily enough for the B♭.

[C]: Get these short phrases to flow and bounce nicely off of the slow rhythm. Watch out for pitch wobbles as well owing to the frequent use of bends on or around the 18th, 19th and 20th frets.

③: There is at the point marked a., a D→F# bend. This wants to be hit with good timing and held a little before being released. Listen to the track and you will see what I mean. In fact this entire theme needs a lush, relaxed kind of feel to it, especially when executing the many bends that make the melody sing out.

PLAY WITH ME

Music by NARADA MICHAEL WALDEN

LOVE IS GREEN

STRUCTURE

[A]: Acoustic guitars double main theme in slow moving beats with various time signatures.
[B]: Repetition of main theme and short, brighter contrasting passage.
[C]: Electric guitar joins to develop brighter passage to climax.
[D]: Variation on [B].
[E]: Ending.

GUITAR SOUND

Beck plays for a change acoustic guitar to enhance the slightly Renaissance atmosphere of the consciously modal theme that dominates the piece. Moreover at least one, if not all, of the guitars on the upper stave is a nylon strung or classical guitar which helps to make musical hints towards an instrument like a lute. He also adds an echo unit of some description on the recording which gives the multi-tracked acoustics an unusually strong presence in an ensemble that would normally drown them out. From section [C] the Stratocaster takes over with a sweetly distorted tone, probably just valve amp overload, and some very delicate playing that combines effortlessly with the acoustics at [D].

PLAYING TIPS

[A]: All of this section is played on acoustic instruments, probably with nylon wound strings. If you're not used to acoustic guitars and nylon strung guitars in particular, you will no doubt find that the approach is far more muscular, for want of a better word, from the point of view of technique. Far more power is needed in the grip of the left hand and the attack of the right hand to get volume, sustain and a good tone, things that on an electric guitar involve the sometimes more abstract if not more complex relationship between guitar/amplifier and an array of electronic gadgets that influence the basic tone. Anyhow, the principles of basic playing techniques apply to both and a simple line like the main theme in this piece won't give any problems but being sure of fingering and positions in advance will prove advantageous on an acoustic.
①: This pull-off and indeed all slurred (i.e. un-picked) notes in this theme should be clearly and decisively sounded.
②: A♭→B♭ glissando. Ditto point ①:.
③: C→E♭ hammer-on. See ①:.

④: The kind of vibrato that you would play on an electric guitar doesn't work very well on a nylon strung guitar as the pitch of nylon strings cannot be very greatly sharpened by bending the strings: a mere one tone bend high up on the fretboard would require you to move the string about two and a half centimetres! So, it's more effective to do this as a classical guitarist would, by simply rocking your left hand to and fro as fast as you can while holding your finger very firmly down on the string, as if you were trying to prevent your finger from sliding up and down between the fretwires. You won't succeed of course as this movement creates the fluctuation of pitch but the intensity of the vibrato comes from the speed with which the hand shakes from side to side, which is then transferred to the string more effectively if the finger on the string is relatively rigid and therefore less likely to flop or slide around. The shaking movement itself is generated more from the left forearm than the wrist.
⑤: This indicates the unison choked notes created by double tracked guitars on the album. All of section [C] is really a climax in the piece which kind of highlights this whole passage. So, pitching and timing these doubled up bends is very important if it's to avoid sounding sloppy. Dud fretwires can also cause the most perfectly executed bends to go wrong. If they are unduly buzzy rub the string over them several times to remove any substances that may have formed on them.
⑥: Another effective choke, very delicately delivered, this time on the 13th fret/1st string from F→A♭ which is left hanging for three beats, then gently released back down to F. It needs a persuasive touch to sound good. N.B. On the original recording Guitar I is mixed to the centre, Guitar II to the right hand channel and Guitar III to the left hand channel.

LOVE IS GREEN

Music by NARADA MICHAEL WALDEN

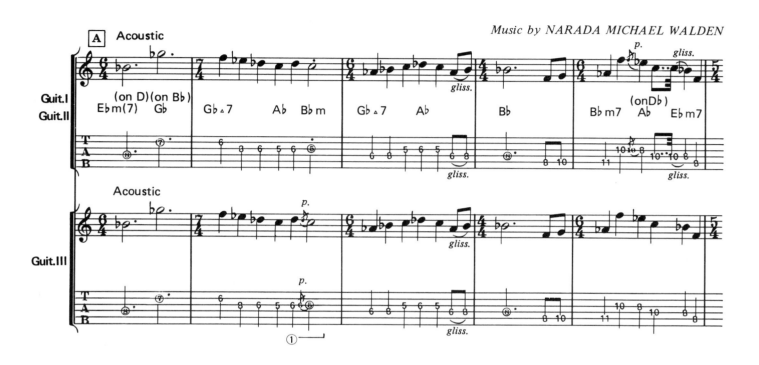

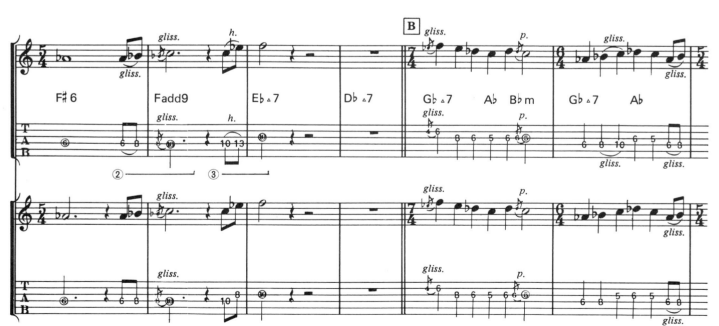

FREEWAY JAM

STRUCTURE

Intro: Solo drums.
[A]: Sketchy improvised passage over rhythm.
[B]: Guitar plays main theme.
[C]: Chorus type contrasting passage, 13 bars long.
[D]: Guitar solo.
[E]: Same as [B].
[F]: Same as [C].
[G]: Ending like [A], over basic rhythm and riff.

GENERAL ASPECTS

Another Strat based number with plenty of happy excesses on the tremolo arm. Apart from that, techniquewise this number is subjected to Beck's usual mixed bag of favourite guitarisms with harmonics, rapid passages of hammer'd and pulled notes and bends that screech and shout rather than weep and wail. Although the album from which this tune comes, "Blow By Blow", saw Beck appear with a radically jazzed up approach to his guitar playing, the appropriately titled 'Freeway Jam' retains a satisfying rawness over a steady boogying 4/4 beat. Rough edged and playful, the guitar wanders all over the fretboard, shooting from the lowest octave up to the narrowest frets as phrases casually disappear into pure guitar noise.

GUITAR SOUND

Basically a beefed up Stratocaster, employing a power booster to thicken and dirty up the sound. If you do this it is advisable to use EQ to bring the piercing treble down a shade as power boosters tend in any case to bump up the higher frequencies which, in conjunction with a Strat, might prove a shade too ear splitting. But with the enhanced sustain, the guitar should end up sounding something like an SG with overdrive which fits this number just right.

PLAYING TIPS

[A]: Fragmented, scattered licks hint at what's to come and create a gradually rising tension in the music. This sounds very improvised

①: This G is just a long held note at the 12th fret with the tremolo arm creating the quaver 'indentations' in it by dropping the pitch a tone and back.

②: A typical Beck phrase created by the tremolo arm. If you take a look at a., the B♭ on the 2nd beat is fingered and the tremolo arm then depressed to lower the pitch down to G. The arm is then released and an F glissando'd up from the 15th fret back to G.

[B]: As the main melody begins after the 4th bar the distortion on the guitar is increased.

③: Another piece of inventive tremolo arm usage: the alternating pairing of G and B♭ is picked but when the G is played the tremolo arm is slightly depressed to make it seem to slide down in pitch and the B♭ is then picked as the tremolo arm rises up to return, creating a tiny upward glissando effect. This creates a very subtle pitch fluctuation on both notes.

④: A couple of points worth mentioning in this descending lick: a. is basically a trill descending in three stages, a series of continuous hammer- ons and pull-offs over the shuffly back beat with each group of 6 or 5 notes to be played in the time of one beat. Index and ring fingers are the best fingers to use here but try to keep the continuity going when you change position from one group to another; b. these two triplet figures want to drag a little on the beat so that stand out with the accent off rather than on the beat and hold the B♭ at the 3rd fret/3rd string with your index finger as you begin the slide up to the B♭ on the 8th fret/4th string with your ring finger and then slide down to G, 3 frets below. Then you repeat this again. This little manoeuvre is definitely a bit tricky. The keypoint is hitting the G accurately.

⑤: This is the same as ④ b. with a variation on the rhythm.

⑥: The run down here contains, with it's F, D♭ and A♭, a blue arpeggio of a D♭ major chord and lends a jazzy air to the solo.

⑦: Eccentric little figure again produced by some imaginative use of the tremolo arm. It's a continuous phrase with staggered, off beat accents that shouldn't be raced through but laid into to express a lazy bluesiness. It might be good to work on this separately before bringing it into the solo.

FREEWAY JAM

Music by MAX MIDDLETON

LADY

STRUCTURE

[A]: Whole band together bring in 2 bar riff.
[B]: Vocal verse over 4 bar pattern (4th time changes chord progression).
[C]: Variation on vocal verse with two 8 bar patterns, the latter with key change and three 2 bar pattern to lead into [D].
[D]: Small drum fill then guitar solo.
[E]: Same riff as [A] to 6 bar drum solo and guitar break.
[F]: Drum solo.
[G]: Same riff as [A] leads to guitar solo and to ending on [A] riff.

GENERAL ASPECTS

For this number we're truly back to rock music with a song from the driving Beck, Bogart, Appice trio. This is a riff based number with some nice chord inversions on the vocal verses, and a catchy and bluesy two part riff on E linking into the vocals, that calls for two finger picking. The guitar solo itself is an amalgamation of hammer'd and pulled phrases delivered with tight, aggressive rock mannerisms. Quite different from the later material.

GUITAR SOUND

On the live album, from which this version is taken, Beck was using a Les Paul with a Sunn amplifier and going for a solid, powerful tone. For this kind of set-up I would just suggest lowering the treble somewhat as these kind of transistor amps, in comparison with a Marshall valve top, tend towards a thin toppiness that does not really suit this number.

PLAYING TIPS

[A]: The chords here are simply E major in the 7th position down to D major two frets below and back again. For the little riff that answers the chords use the middle finger and the ring finger.
①: These powerful tremolo'd chords need to be executed with fast strumming strokes in the right hand and a vibrato in the left hand to create the steam train wailing sound which then comes to climax on the three high B/D chords at the 19th fret.
②: Play an E9 in the 7th position for these chords and slide the 3rd and 4th strings up from a semitone below to get the glissando effect. All of this passage is based around

this E9 chord, which if you do not know it is: middle finger on the 7th fret/5th string, index finger on the 6th fret/4th string and a ring finger bar at the 7th fret across the top 3 strings. This will make the following slide up on the 2nd and 3rd strings from 6th to 7th fret quite easy. As you can guess, the rhythm of this chord riff is more important than hitting any exact sequence of notes. Lay on the beat and staccato the first note(s) on the first beat of each bar.
③: Effective little chord glissando over the E harmony, sliding down to D and back as in the opening chords.
④: To play this descending lick of continuous pull-offs, you have to keep in the 12th position with your index finger either barring at or fretting all the notes that fall on the 12th fret.
⑤: Simple E major arpeggio with harmonics all on the 6th string. You could play this across the strings, but although the harmony would be stronger with more notes ringing together, the rhythmic attack would be lost. Beck often uses this kind of device in his playing.
⑥: A small phrase built around an E blues scale at the 12th position. The 1st string should be played with the index finger and the 2nd string with the ring finger. The second bar contains a repeated G→G# bend.
⑦: The repeated 3 and 2 note figures in these two bars are played by continuously pulling-off and hammering-on with the left hand; the right hand only picks the first note. It could sound fine when picked as well but staying on the beat will be slightly more demanding.
N.B. There is a tricky little variation on the three note E riff that runs into the singing verse, where a bass note is added underneath. If you take a look at the last 8 bars just before the 'D.S.', between the two drum breaks, you will see this figure lasting 6 bars. You need to mute the bottom E string in the right hand and play these open E's with the pick while playing the D and G strings with your middle finger on the right hand. This could feel awkward at first as it is basically a two part riff, unusual in rock guitar but not in acoustic guitar based American country blues. The hard thing is that the E bass must keep a solid and regular beat while the little riff dances above. The last E after the open 3rd string is always the hardest to keep on the beat.

LADY

Words & Music by BECK, BOGERT, APPICE, HITCHINGS & FRENCH

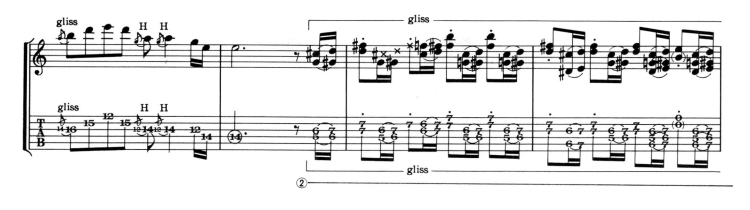

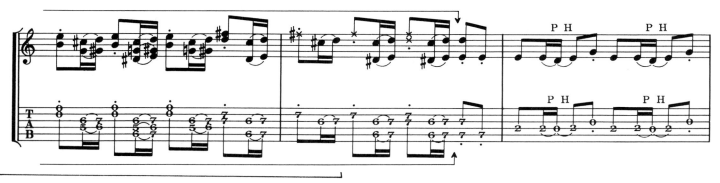

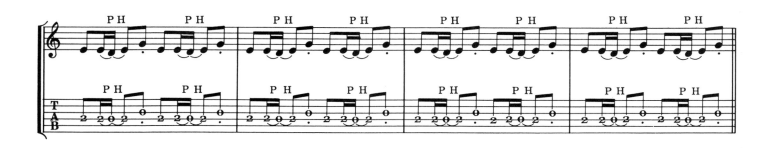

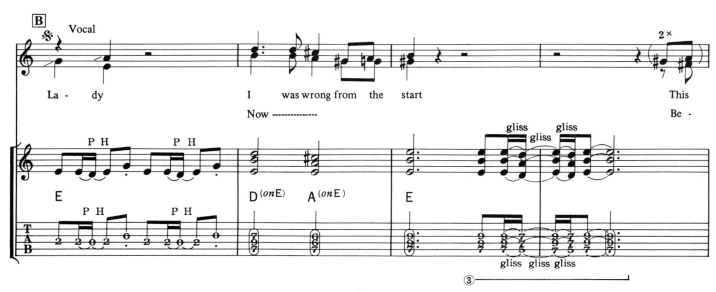

La - dy   I   was wrong from the   start   This

Now ----------------   Be -

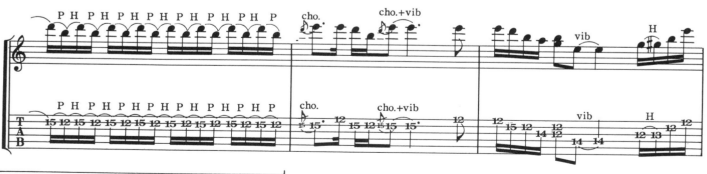

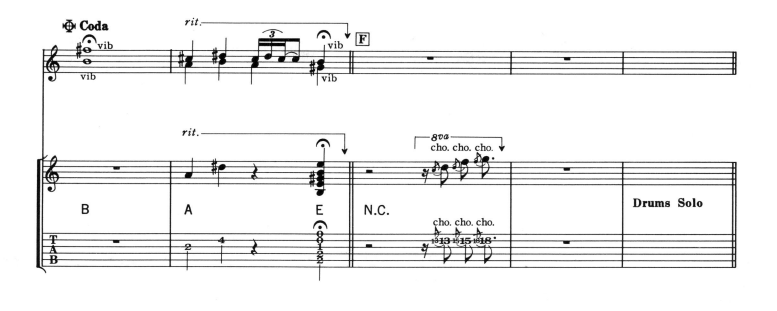

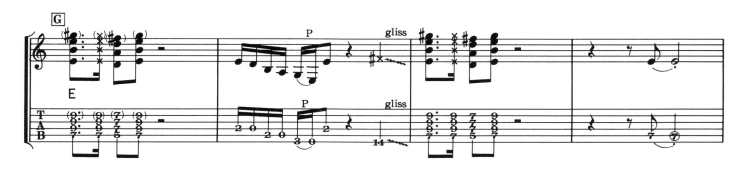

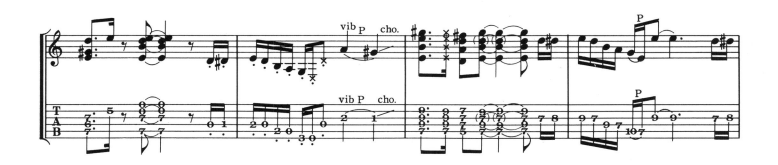

HIGHWAYS

STRUCTURE

[A]: 8 bar intro chords with guitar soloing above.
[B]: Vocals begin with key change to F.
[C]: Guitar solo.
[D] or coda: guitar solo.
[E]: Piano solo on Dm7-B♭ m7 and fade out.

GENERAL ASPECTS

Aside from some neat tremolo arm and a little slide guitar there is nothing particularly outstanding in the guitar part of 'Highways'. For this slow ballad Beck curiously throws in some rather too obvious rock licks delivered with a frantic attack that seem frequently at odds with the essentially jazzy harmony of the vocal verse and the electric piano soloing on which the song ends. It does nonetheless contain some very solid and confident phrase building as well as showing Beck's mastery of his instrument. It also seems to reveal some of the stylistic watershed that saw him later develop a genuine synthesis between his R&B roots and his leanings towards jazz.

GUITAR SOUND

At the time this was recorded Beck often used a combination of Stratocaster and Marshall amps. In this song there are some nifty changes of tone, often just a result of switching over pickups, as when he goes from the solo at the beginning of the piece into the vocal lines, switching from 3rd to 1st pickups in the 11th bar for the back-up work. However some chord passages sound as though they are played through the middle pickup. The guitar solo that follows has yet again a different sound to the lead playing in the introductory bars. The tone is less harsh with less sustain, coming probably from the 1st pickup. All in all, mood changes, key changes and even chord changes spur Beck into altering his sound to add a contrasting texture that emphasises variations of harmony or form. To appreciate this it is only necessary to listen closely to his playing on the albums and experiment yourself with this principle in mind.

PLAYING TIPS

[A]: This lead work has a bizarre urgency about it that tends to make the rhythm fairly rigid. He uses the 3rd or bridge pickup with what sounds like a heavy duty plectrum, one of the thick ones. A hard pick will naturally produce a thicker tone but this suits the strictly rock guitar phrases here.

①: This series of bent notes is based around a common enough device of bending up to a note fingered on the adjacent string: play the D at the 10th fret/1st string with the index finger and bend the C→D on the 13th fret/2nd string with the ring finger and be sure to come in just off the beat.

②: A combination of various basic techniques with chokes, hammers, pull- offs and vibrato. Like ①: this passage is based on a D scale in the 10th position with a little hammer-on/pull-off leading into a rapid slide up to a D bend.

③: Another little idiomatic rock lick. Beginners might find it tricky to keep the first 4 notes on the beat as they are made by picking the G and then bending up to the A, then releasing the bend down to G again, pulling-off to F. In other words only the first note is picked. If it causes any trouble, just practise it alone over a slow beat until you can feel the timing under each note.

④: A nice chord voicing of a minor 7th chord on the backward arpeggio. The fingering requires a big stretch as although the first 3 notes of G, D and B♭ can be simply barred with the index finger across the top 3 strings at the 3rd fret, the A on the 4th string must be reached with the little finger. This fingering should also be used for the B♭ m7 in the following bar. Getting the up stroke of the pick across the chord to sound smooth might also take a little practice.

⑤: Finger this repeated phrase of continuous hammer-ons and pull-offs with the index finger at the 10th fret/1st string, the ring finger at 12th fret and the little finger at the 13th fret. Aim for clarity, as ever, when playing continuously slurred passages.

⑥: Right at the beginning of the bar is an F♮ 'acciatura' which has to be played very quickly, being slid into the F# that follows, as soon as it is sounded, all on the same beat. This is a common enough device in rock or any style of music and a quick listen to the album will make this clear straight away.

HIGHWAYS

Words & Music by JEFF BECK

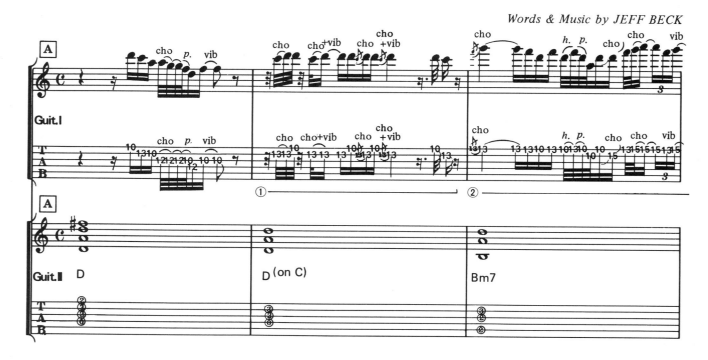

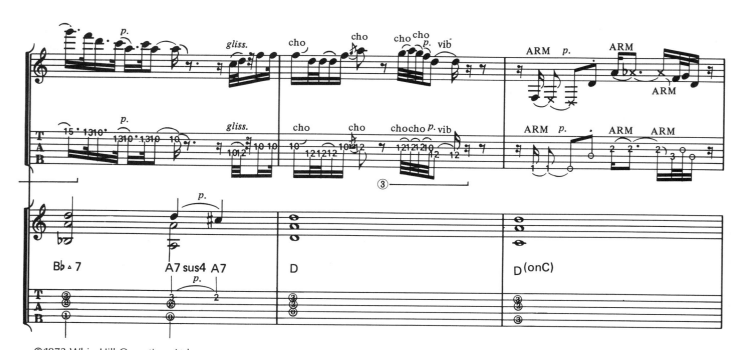

VOCAL

oh I been

D.S.

DEFINITELY MAYBE

STRUCTURE

Intro: Piano chords and drums for 4 bars.
[A]: Guitar entry with theme.
[B]: Guitar II entry with unison in 3rds on theme of [A].
[C]: Guitar I alone continues theme.
[D]: Solo from Guitar III for 14 bars.
[E]&[F]: Continuation and climax of guitar solo to main hook of song.
[G]: Twin slide guitars play variation on [B].
[H]: Variation on main theme from 3 guitars.
[I]: Theme of Guitar I.
[J]: Electric piano solo and fade out.

GENERAL ASPECTS

The most striking features of this brooding, sad waltz with it's Spaghetti Western hook, are the clear, simple melody and the beautiful slide playing with which it is delivered. The core of the guitar tone is the mixture of wah-wah pedal and slide guitar. If you are not used to slide playing, three main points worth considering are muting, accuracy of pitch and getting a good tone. Muting is obviously very important owing to the phenomenal amount of sustain created by using a bottleneck. It's often more convenient to use a spare finger on your left hand, maybe the index finger, than your right hand, although the late and great slide player Duane Allman, as a finger picker, would usually use his right hand. So, see what works best. Accuracy will depend a lot on how difficult the melody is and whether it requires big jumps in position: if all the notes can be found on two adjacent strings then it will suit this style better than having to cross the strings constantly. So, thinking a little about position can be useful. It is also better not to rely too much on the fretwires to find the notes. Using your ears as a guide to hitting the correct pitch, rather like a violinist, is half the art of developing a good ability to play slide guitar. One good way of getting the feel of this technique is to practice on scales. This gets you used to cross-stringing, position changes and playing on one string without sounding the others. Finally, getting an even pressure on the bar is very important for a nice tone as well eliminating any string rattle against the sides of the metal bar. The amount of pressure that you put on the bar will also affect the tone quality.

GUITAR SOUND

The guitar set-up is relatively simple. A Strat/Marshall combination with a bottleneck and a wah-wah pedal will produce the basic guitar tone on the album. To thicken up the sound a little, a power booster with EQ added could prove effective if the natural valve overload of the amp does not suffice. As you can hear from the track, the wah-wah is used in quite a subtle way to shape and add expression to phrases rather than as a characteristic sound in the song.

PLAYING TIPS

[A]: This is the first theme with the first 3 bars played on the 2nd string. The first two phrases consist of 3 bars each and it is best to get as many notes of any one phrase as possible to fall on the same string, rather than breaking them up in the middle with a string change. This will make for greater smoothness and facilitate your control over the slide.
①: One of the many points into the melody, where Beck adds vibrato to his slide playing. Bear in mind to listen for the pitch rather than to just aim for the right fretwires.
②: A typical but straightforward example of a tricky leap on the same string: the G→E slide of 3 frets on the 2nd string is followed by a big slide up to the 12th fret. It is very easy to make a botch of this kind of thing and miss all the pitches, blur the phrase and/or overshoot the long slide up to the B at the 12th fret.
③: Here, on these 4 ascending notes, is an occasion that calls for good muting as, if you listen to the track, they all have to be played with a clear pause in between, like a half staccato. You have to stop the held over D note from the former bar and then mute each of the following notes in turn. As the high G note at the end has a climactic role, don't cut it off too abruptly. Let it sing out for a good crotchet beat before stopping it.

DEFINITELY MAYBE

Music by *JEFF BECK*

Sub-published by B. Feldman & Co. Ltd., Trading as Equator Music, London WC2H 0EA

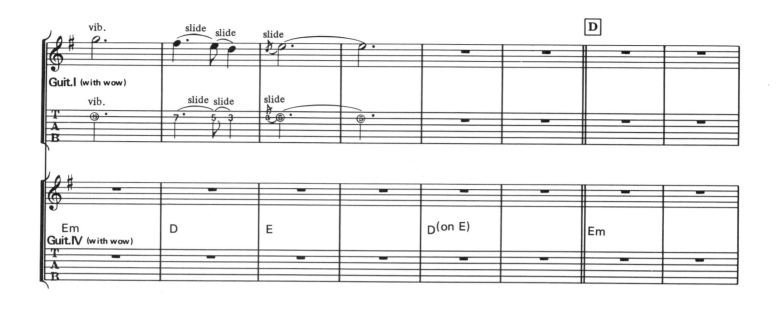

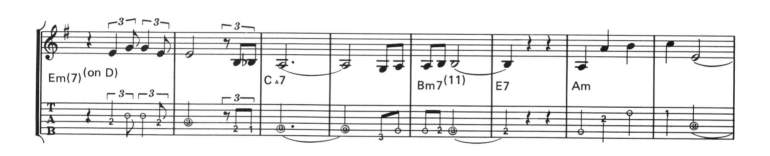

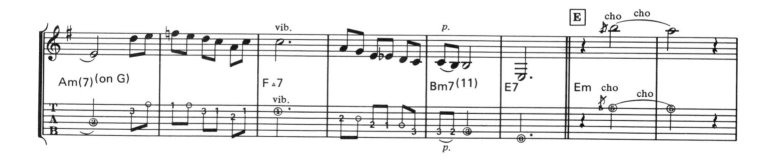

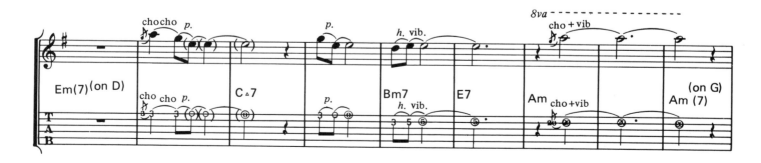

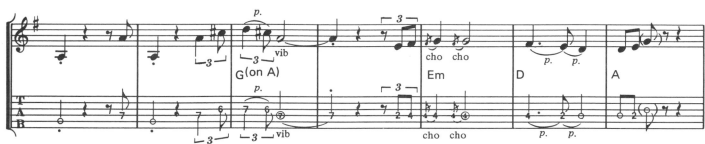

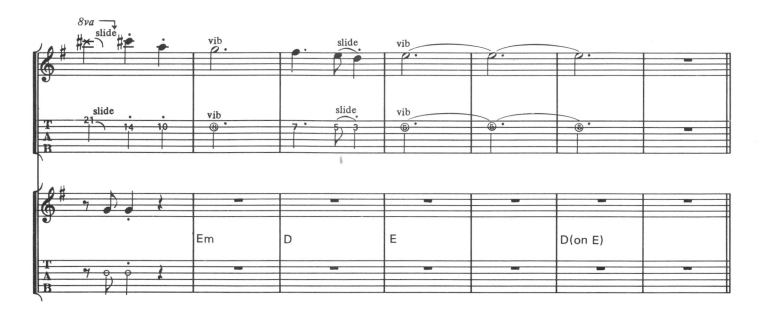

JAILHOUSE ROCK

STRUCTURE

Intro: Guitar and drums play chord riff 2x.
Ⓐ&Ⓑ: Vocal verse and chorus.
Ⓒ&Ⓓ: Guitar solo.
Ⓔ: Acoustic piano solo.
Ⓕ: Same as Ⓐ but guitar plays phrases with and under lead vocal lines.
Ⓖ: Vocal chorus.
Ⓗ: Guitar solo interspersed with vocals.
Ⓘ: Guitar solo.
Ⓙ: Same as Ⓖ with guitar licks underneath to fade out.

GENERAL ASPECTS

A fair amount of tremolo arm is called for in the solo for some big, brash note bends as well as arm'd down trills, a device that often surfaces in Beck's rock improvisation. There's also a lot of accented slides that imitate the effect of a tremolo arm, especially those on the lower strings, which take advantage of the distortion to create some screeching downward glissandos. At times it is difficult to tell whether this sound has come from a downward slide or depressing the tremolo arm. So this is yet another piece for a Fender Stratocaster and preferably one that, like Beck's own, has a 'synchronised tremolo unit' to stop the guitar from going too wildly out of tune.

GUITAR SOUND

Although Beck often used a Les Paul as well at this time, everything on this number points to a Strat and Marshall pairing. A fuzz box also surfaces from time to time, most notably during the guitar solo along with a little controlled feedback. If you find that you are unable to get feedback because of being obliged to play at low volume, try using a power booster on the guitar which will increase the input signal and therefore enhance the potential for feedback. And bear in mind that the angle or direction in which you actually face the speakers when playing can affect the frequency of the feedback.

PLAYING TIPS

Ⓐ: Anyone familiar with this song - surely nearly everyone - shouldn't need telling that these chords have to really lay into the beat in a way that makes it drag slightly. When you transcribe it onto the score it comes out as falling just off of the last beat in the bar as a dotted quaver.

①: Although it is written out as a 3 note chord you could try adding an A on top as it brings the chord out well.

②: This is one of those downward glissandos that have the effect of a tremolo arm.

③: A small lick but containing a nice tension from the 7th and flattened 3rd which needs to come across. It's wise to finger the E♭ on the 3rd string and the A♭ on the 2nd string at the same time and then mute the E♭ just before you bend the A♭ slightly.

④: This one and a half tone bend from F→A♭ occurs at the 15th fret/4th string, not the easiest of strings to bend but unfortunately it just doesn't sound as good elsewhere on the fretboard.

⑤: Repeated semiquaver figure containing several hammer-ons and pull-offs. Basically it's just two notes, E♭ and C, fingered with the index and ring or little fingers.

⑥: Nice example of a bend coupled with vibrato, comfortably picked up on the 2nd string where there is less tension and more space than on the top E string.

⑦: A piece of destructive phrasing with the tremolo arm. You have to execute the G→D♭ slide right up to the 21st fret and then bend up a tone before arming down on the open 1st string.

⑧: This device has already been explained in other songs: just trill with the index and ring fingers on the 13th and 16th frets of the 2nd string while depressing the tremolo arm to lower the pitch.

⑨: This is a combination of tremolo arm and feedback. To get the bottom E♭ finger an F on the 1st fret/6th string and press the tremolo arm down to lower the pitch a tone, returning it again while picking the F. For the feedback, experiment with different positions between the guitar and the speakers.

JAILHOUSE ROCK

Words & Music by JERRY LEIDER & MIKE STOLLER

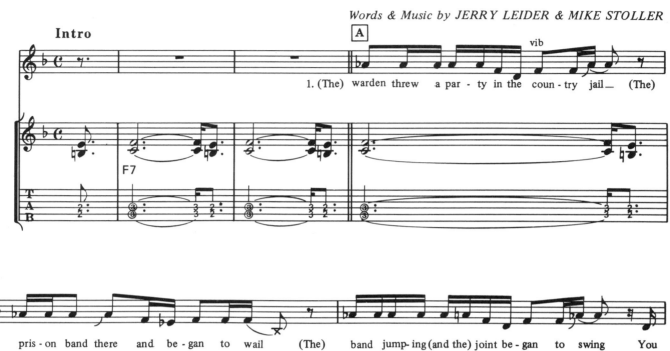

1. (The) warden threw a par-ty in the coun-try jail___ (The)

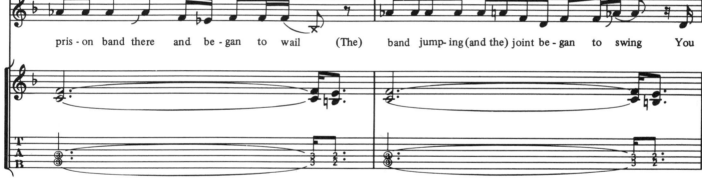

pris-on band there and be-gan to wail (The) band jump-ing (and the) joint be-gan to swing You

should've heard the knock down jail-birds sing Let's rock Ev-'ry-bo-dy le-t's rock (Every-

body) in whole cell ___ block ___ was danc - ing to the Jail - house Rock ___ yeah! ___ (the)

Printed in England
Panda Press · Haverhill Suffolk • 12/91

SELECTED

DISCOGRAPHY

OVER UNDER SIDEWAYS DOWN
(The Yardbirds)

((SIDE ONE))
Lost Women
Over, Under, Sideways Down
The Nuzz Are Blue
I Can't Make Your Way
Rack My Mind
Farewell

((SIDE TWO))
Hot House Of Omagarashid
Jeff's Boogie
He's Always There
Turn Into Earth
What Do You Want
Ever Since The World Began

TRUTH

((SIDE ONE))
Shapes Of Things
Let Me Love You
Morning Dew
You Shook Me
Ol' Man River

((SIDE TWO))
Greensleeves
Rock My Plimsoul
Beck's Bolero
Blues De Luxe
I Ain't Superstitious

COSA NOSTRA BECK-OLA

((SIDE ONE))
All Shook Up
Spanish Boots
Girl From Mill Valley
★ Jailhouse Rock

((SIDE TWO))
Plynth(Water Down The Drain)
Hangman's Knee
Rice Pudding

ROUGH AND READY
(Jeff Beck Group)

((SIDE ONE))
+ Got The Feeling
Situation
Short Business
Max's Tune

((SIDE TWO))
I've Been Used
+ New Ways ~ Train Train
Jody

JEFF BECK GROUP

((SIDE ONE))
+ Ice Cream Cakes
Glad All Over
Tonight I'll Be Staying Here With You
Sugar Cane
I Can't Give Back The Love I Feel For You

((SIDE TWO))
Going Down
I Got To Have A Song
★ Highways
★ Definitely Maybe

BECK, BOGERT & APPICE

((SIDE ONE))
Black Cat Moan
Lady
Oh To Love You
Superstition

((SIDE TWO))
Sweet Sweet Surrender
Why Should I Care
Lose Myself With You
Livin' Alone
I'm So Proud

BECK, BOGERT & APPICE LIVE

((SIDE ONE))
Superstition
Lose Myself With You
+ Jeff's Boogie

((SIDE TWO))
Going Down
Boogie
Morning Dew

((SIDE THREE))
Sweet Sweet Surrender
Living Alone
I'm So Proud
★ Lady

((SIDE FOUR))
Black Cat Moan
Why Should I Care
Plynth~Shotgun(Medley)

BLOW BY BLOW

((SIDE ONE))
+ You Know What I Mean
She's A Woman
Constipated Duck
+ Air Blower
+ Scatterbrain

((SIDE TWO))
Cause We've Ended As Lovers
Thelonius
★ Freeway Jam
Diamond Dust

WIRED

((SIDE ONE))
+ Led Boots
★ Come Dancing
Goodbye Pork Pie Hat
+ Head For Backstage Pass

((SIDE TWO))
★ Blue Wind
★ Sophie
★ Play With Me
★ Love Is Green

JEFF BECK / WITH THE JAN HAMMER GROUP LIVE

((SIDE ONE))
Freeway Jam
Earth(Still Our Only Home)
She's A Woman
Full Moon Boogie

((SIDE TWO))
Darkness/Earth In Search Of A Sun
Scatterbrain
Blue Wind

+ Jeff Beck 1 - Super Rock Guitarist
★ Jeff Beck 2 - Super Rock Guitarist